GREEK COOKBOOK

70 Recipes for Preparing at Home Traditional Food from Greece

---

Maki Blanc

© **Copyright 2021 by Maki Blanc - All rights reserved.**

This document is geared towards providing exact and reliable information in regards to the topic and issue covered. The publication is sold with the idea that the publisher is not required to render accounting, officially permitted, or otherwise, qualified services. If advice is necessary, legal or professional, a practiced individual in the profession should be ordered.

- From a Declaration of Principles which was accepted and approved equally by a Committee of the American Bar Association and a Committee of Publishers and Associations.

It is not legal in any way to reproduce, duplicate, or transmit any part of this document in either electronic means or in printed format. Recording of this publication is strictly prohibited and any storage of this document is not allowed unless with written permission from the publisher. All rights reserved.

The information provided herein is stated to be truthful and consistent, in that any liability, in terms of inattention or otherwise, by any usage or abuse of any policies, processes, or directions contained within is the solitary and utter responsibility of the recipient reader. Under no circumstances will any legal responsibility or blame be held against the publisher for any reparation, damages, or monetary loss due to the information herein, either directly or indirectly.

Respective authors own all copyrights not held by the publisher.

The information herein is offered for informational purposes solely, and is universal as so. The presentation of the information is without contract or any type of guarantee assurance.

The trademarks that are used are without any consent, and the publication of the trademark is without permission or backing by the trademark owner. All trademarks and brands within this book are for clarifying purposes only and are the owned by the owners themselves, not affiliated with this document.

Contents

INTRODUCTION 8

CHAPTER 1: GREEK BREAKFAST RECIPES 10

1.1 Greek Breakfast Egg Skillet with Feta and Sautéed Veggies 10

1.2 Greek Breakfast Bagel 11

1.3 Cliff's Greek Breakfast Pitas 12

1.4 Greek Breakfast Egg Muffins 13

1.5 Greek Scrambled Eggs 14

1.6 Lemon Hummus Toast with Feta & Eggs 15

1.7 Greek Breakfast Wrap 16

1.8 Greek Potato Breakfast Skillet 16

1.9 Greek Eggs Kayana 18

1.10 Greek Wrap Breakfast with Green Pepper, Tomato, Feta & Olives 19

CHAPTER 2: GREEK APPETIZERS AND SNACKS 21

2.1 Healthy Greek Appetizer Platter 21

2.2 Greek Salad Skewers 22

2.3 Greek-inspired Snack Board 23

2.4 Greek Garden Appetizer 24

2.5 Feta and Greek Yogurt Pita Appetizer 25

2.6 Greek Layer Dip 26

2.7 Cheesy Greek Swirls 27

2.8 Cool and Tangy Greek Snacks 28

2.9 Greek Savory Snacks 28

2.10 Greek Burrito Snack Wrap 29

2.11 Greek Salad Snack Skewers 30

2.12 Saganaki Recipe 31

2.13 Greek Stuffed Cucumber Bites 33

2.14 Greek Tortilla Pinwheels 33

CHAPTER 3: GREEK LUNCH RECIPES 35

3.1 Skordalia 35

3.2 Greek Chicken Rice Bowl 36

3.3 Quick and Healthy Greek Salmon Salad 37

3.4 Mediterranean Orzo Salad Recipe 39

3.5 Melitzanosalata Recipe (Greek Eggplant Dip) 40

3.6 Greek Salad with Chicken 42

3.7 Greek Chicken and Potatoes 43

3.8 Quick-Roasted Tomatoes with Garlic and Thyme 44

3.9 Greek-Style Baked Feta Recipe 45

3.10 Greek Bowls with Roasted Garbanzo Beans 46

CHAPTER 4: GREEK DINNER RECIPES 49

4.1 Grilled Eggplant Pita Pizzas 49

4.2 Garlic-Grilled Chicken with Pesto Zucchini Ribbons..........50

4.3 Grilled Eggplant with Feta Relish......................................52

4.4 Greek Beef Pitas 54

4.5 Greek Brown and Wild Rice Bowls 55

4.6 Greek Sheet Pan Chicken Dinner 55

4.7 Grecian Chicken 56

4.8 Greek Tilapia 58

4.9 Greek-Style Stuffed Peppers..58

4.10 Lemony Greek Beef and Vegetables................................60

CHAPTER 5: GREEK SALADS....................................62

5.1 Greek Salad with Chicken...62

5.2 Greek Salad Recipe with Lemon Dressing........................63

5.3 Greek Salad with Edamame 63

5.4 Chopped Greek Salad...64

5.5 Greek Pasta Salad 65

5.6 Ladolemono Greek Salad Dressing 66

5.7 Greek Salad with Lettuce and Lemon Garlic Dressing........67

5.8 Athens Greek Salad..68

5.9 Greek Salad with Homemade Vinaigrette 69

5.10 Quick and Light Greek Salad..69

CHAPTER 6: GREEK SOUPS AND SIDES 71

6.1 Avgolemono: Greek Lemon Chicken Soup 71

6.2 Kakavia 72

6.3 Kotosoupa 73

6.4 Pattas 74

6.5 Fasolada 75

6.6 Revithia 75

6.7 Youvarlakia 77

6.8 Psarosoupa 78

6.9 Magiritsa 79

6.10 Traditional Greek Lentil Soup 80

CHAPTER 7: GREEK DESSERTS 82

7.1 Traditional Greek Galaktoboureko 82

7.2 Baklava Recipe 83

7.3 Greek Honey Cake 84

7.4 Loukoumades 85

7.5 Greek Skillet Orange Fillo Cake 86

7.6 Fried Greek Pastry with Honey and Nuts 87

CONCLUSION 89

Introduction

Greek food is part of Greece's history and is present in old pictures and writings. Its thriftiness defined ancient Greek culinary and was based on the "Mediterranean triangle": grain, olive, and wine, with seldom consumed meat and more popular fish. Greek food, coupled with hundreds of years of practice, includes some of the area's wealthiest flavors to produce endless mouth-watering meals. While Greek cuisine has many variations, the roots of Greek food stay the same.

Greece is grateful to be one of the world's most delicate ecosystems, one where abundant sunlight helps grow some of the tastiest vegetables and fruits. Since Greece, fresh ingredients from field to meadow to farm to ocean are wonderful in their very own right. Greek cuisine has developed so that the purity of such fresh foods is innately valued. Greek food, a food culture whose central tenet is that nutrition should be prepared as near its natural form. It is not a portion of food with a repertoire of intricate sauces or demanding methods. It is not a meal that appreciates culinary expressions. The bulk of techniques are simple and instant.

Being that Greece is quite close to Istanbul, it has benefited from being a global trading center. Thousands of great herbs and spices also appeared in Greece. As well as that, Greece had to play with some fresh vegetables! How Turkish and Greek food is so close is explained by the fact that it was a world trading period, with Constantinople in the middle. Greek cuisine also contains some amazing cakes and plenty of robust sauces, delicious appetizers, and decent wine.

Greece is a small nation with a remarkably varied landscape, as expressed in its local table. Island cuisine is available for mountainous cooking, Peloponnesian food, Cretan cuisine, and more.

Like the general gamut of raw materials, the taste palette varies by region. Northern Greek cuisine appears, for instance, to be spicier than island cuisine. Cooking on the mainland appears to be healthier.

"Greek Cookbook" includes a wide variety of different foods from Greek cuisine. It has seven chapters. The first chapter is about the breakfast recipes from Greek cuisine. While Chapters two, three, and four are about snacks, appetizers, and lunch and dinner recipes of Greek cuisine. Chapter five, six, seven are about salad, soups, sides, and desserts. Start reading this book and enjoy Greek food with more health benefits.

Chapter 1: Greek Breakfast Recipes

1.1 Greek Breakfast Egg Skillet with Feta and Sautéed Veggies

Cooking Time: 15 minutes
Serving Size: 4
Ingredients:
- 4 large eggs
- ¼ cup feta cheese
- 1 teaspoon garlic powder
- 1 teaspoon oregano
- 12 cups baby spinach
- Salt and pepper to taste
- 1 tablespoon olive oil
- 1 medium red bell pepper
- 1 medium onion

Method:
1. Drizzle vegetable oil into a large nonstick saucepan over medium heat.
2. Sauté the onions and peppers for about 4-5 minutes, or until they are tender.
3. Season to taste with garlic powder, marjoram, and salt, and black pepper.
4. Cook, occasionally stirring, until the spinach has wilted, around 1-2 minutes.
5. Serve the sautéed vegetables on four plates, via an egg cooked to order on top of each plate.
6. Before serving, top each dish with a tablespoon of cheddar cheese.

1.2 Greek Breakfast Bagel

Cooking Time: 5 minutes

Serving Size: 2

Ingredients:
- ½ cup baby spinach
- 1 tablespoon crumbled feta cheese
- 1 Plain Bagel
- 1 teaspoon olive oil
- 8 cherry tomatoes, halved
- 2 eggs
- Freshly ground pepper
- Pinch each salt

Method:
1. Beat the eggs, spice, and peppers together; set them aside.
2. Heat the olive oil over medium-high heat in a frying pan; fry the vegetables for about four minutes, or begin to soften.
3. Insert spinach; fry for around two minutes until it is wilted moderately.
4. Put in beaten egg; fry for three or four minutes or until soft curds begin to develop from the egg mixture.
5. Mix in cheese from the feta. Spoon over the halves of bagels.

1.3 Cliff's Greek Breakfast Pitas

Cooking Time: 1 hour 35 minutes
Serving Size: 8

Ingredients:
- 1 pound thick-cut bacon

Tzatziki Sauce
- 8 eggs
- Ground black pepper
- 1 white onion
- ½ cup olive oil
- 1 (16 ounces) bag mix greens
- 3 Roma tomatoes
- 2 cups plain Greek yogurt
- 1 ½ pounds breakfast sausage
- 4 pita bread rounds
- 2 cucumbers
- 2 teaspoons ground white pepper
- Salt to taste
- 3 cloves garlic

Method:
1. Heat the oven to 400 degrees Fahrenheit.
2. Organize bacon on the paper in a thin layer.
3. Place in the preheated oven and cook for 10 to 15 minutes before the optimal amount of crispiness is achieved.
4. Move bacon to a lined plate of clean cloth to soak and retain bacon fat.
5. Place it in a bowl of Greek yogurt.
6. Halve 1 cucumber and grind part of it into the yogurt.
7. To create tzatziki dip, whisk in garlic powder, white pepper, and salt.
8. The leftover cucumber can be sliced into thin pieces and put aside.
9. Over moderate flame, heat a skillet.
10. Insert the sausage; roast and stir for five minutes, until golden brown.
11. Switch to a pan.

12. Move the bacon fat over medium-high heat to a pan.
13. Insert pita rounds; roast on each side once lightly browned, about 30 seconds. Absorb on towels.
14. Cover with sausage and bacon from each pita.
15. On each pita, arrange tzatziki dip, spring mixture, Roma tomato, cucumber pieces, and onions.
16. In a shallow pan, add the remaining tablespoon of oil.
17. Crack in one egg; cook approximately 1½ minutes per side once set but still tender.
18. Place the egg on a baked pita top.
19. Continue with the oil and eggs available.

1.4 Greek Breakfast Egg Muffins

Cooking Time: 30 minutes
Serving Size: 12

Ingredients:
- ¾ cup tomatoes
- ⅓ cup pitted black olives
- 1 cup crumbled Feta cheese
- ⅓ cup cream heavy cream
- 10 eggs

Method:
1. Set the oven to 350°F. In a muffin tray, put sixteen muffin trays.
2. Beat and combine the eggs with all the other components.
3. On a muffin plate, load into muffin lining and bake in the oven center for twenty minutes until crispy and hardened.

1.5 Greek Scrambled Eggs

Cooking Time: 15 minutes
Serving Size: 2
   Ingredients:
   - 1 cup cherry tomatoes
   - Toast or toasted pita bread
   - ½ medium yellow onion
   - 6 ounces baby spinach
   - ¼ teaspoon black pepper
   - 1 tablespoon olive oil
   - 10 large eggs
   - ¼ cup milk
   - ½ teaspoon fine salt
   - ¾ cup crumbled feta cheese

Method:
1. Beat the eggs, feta, dairy, half teaspoon salt, and ¼ teaspoon spice in a large mixing bowl to merge; set it aside.
2. Place the butter in a pan nonstick deep fryer or stainless cast iron pan over medium-high heat until glinting.
3. Insert the onions, sprinkle with salt, and simmer for about five minutes, stirring periodically, until softened.
4. Add the spinach once thoroughly wilted, and any moisture has evaporated, flipping continuously for around three minutes.
5. Lower the heat to moderate and put in the combination of the eggs.
6. Let sit uninterrupted, 2 minutes, before the eggs begin to set around the sides.
7. Move the placed eggs from the sides towards the middle using a slotted spoon.
8. Back into a layer, scatter the raw eggs.

9. Repeat for a cumulative cooking time of around four to six minutes, moving the prepared eggs from the sides to the middle every thirty seconds until almost complete.
10. Drop the heat from the skillet and place the tomatoes in it.
11. Serve with bread or baked pita bread right away.

1.6 Lemon Hummus Toast with Feta & Eggs

Cooking Time: 30 minutes
Serving Size: 4

Ingredients:
- 2 teaspoons parsley
- Pinch of sweet paprika
- 8 teaspoons Greek feta
- 2 eggs boiled
- 4 slices sourdough bread
- 2 firm-ripe tomatoes
- 8 tablespoons lemon hummus

Method:
1. The eggs should be peeled and quartered.
2. On the buttered toast, scatter the avocado hummus.
3. Over the hummus, arrange the tomato slices.
4. Serve with feta crumbles on top.
5. On top of that, put the eggs.
6. Offer with a garnish of parsley and parmesan.

1.7 Greek Breakfast Wrap

Cooking Time: 15 minutes
Serving Size: 4
  Ingredients:
  - 2 tablespoon Kalamata olives
  - 3 tablespoon feta cheese
  - 4 scrambled eggs
  - 4 cherry tomatoes
  - 2 tablespoon tzatziki sauce
  - 2 tortillas

Method:
1. Place the tortillas on a floured work surface and scatter the tzatziki down the middle of each one.
2. Scrambled eggs, onions, olives, and parmesan cheese are uniformly distributed on top.
3. Fold the tortillas' bottoms out over the stuffing, then pull in the sides and roll them up securely.

1.8 Greek Potato Breakfast Skillet

Cooking Time: 20 minutes
Serving Size: 4
  Ingredients:
  - 2 tablespoons flat-leaf parsley
  - 4 eggs
  - ¾ ounce Kalamata olives
  - 3 tablespoons feta cheese
  - ¼ teaspoon kosher salt
  - 3 cloves garlic
  - 2 cups spinach
  - ¼ teaspoon ground pepper
  - 4 teaspoons olive oil
  - 12 grape or cherry tomatoes

- 1 pound package potatoes

Method:
1. Prepare the potato as per the box instructions, stirring the spice package with two tablespoons of olive oil.
2. Over moderate flame, heat a large sauté pan.
3. Stir in the potatoes, then simmer for two minutes.
4. Mix in the tomatoes and simmer until the potatoes begin to yellow and the tomatoes begin to peel, stirring periodically.
5. To one bottom of the plate, move the tomatoes and potatoes and add the remaining two teaspoons of olive oil.
6. Transfer the cloves and spinach to the olive oil.
7. Cook for about two minutes, stirring continuously until the spinach is wilting.
8. Free from the heat. Mix in the pine nuts, coriander, and feta.
9. Cook the eggs, crispy side up, in a small nonstick pan while the potatoes and tomato combination is frying.
10. Divide the mixture of potatoes into four plates.
11. Cover with a fried egg for each meal.

1.9 Greek Eggs Kayana

Cooking Time: 6 minutes
Serving Size: 4

Ingredients:
- Sea salt
- Freshly ground pepper
- 3 tablespoon extra-virgin olive oil
- Dry oregano
- 2 large tomatoes

- 2 cloves garlic
- 6 eggs organic free-range

For Serving
- Chili pepper flakes
- Feta cheese

Method:
1. In a saucepan, stir in the olive oil.
2. Stir in the diced cloves and sauté for two minutes over medium-high heat.
3. Put some tomatoes. With salt and black pepper, mix.
4. Spray 1 tablespoon of oregano over everything.
5. Stir in the tomatoes and fry for 5-6 minutes, stirring regularly.
6. To the pot, add the egg mixture and gently blend it.
7. Stir in the tomatoes and egg combination three times.
8. Cook the eggs according to the texture you like.
9. Serve instantly with a swirl of hot chili flakes, a crumbled feta cheese, or both.
10. If you like, add some chopped herbs, such as mint or basil.

1.10 Greek Wrap Breakfast with Green Pepper, Tomato, Feta & Olives

Cooking Time: 15 minutes
Serving Size: 4

Ingredients:
- Oregano, dried
- Salt
- Extra virgin olive oil
- Black pepper
- 1 shallot

- 2 tomatoes
- ½ cup Kalamata olives pitted
- 4 large flour tortillas
- ½ (4 oz.) feta cheese
- 1 green bell pepper
- 8 eggs

Method:
1. In a medium mixing dish, finely dice the tomato and bell pepper.
2. Transfer the olives, onions, and bell pepper to the bowl after halving them down the middle.
3. Chop and mince the spring onions, then blend them with canola oil, oregano, and pepper in a mixing bowl. To mix, stir all together.
4. Over moderate flame, preheat a nonstick skillet.
5. In a medium mixing cup, break the eggs.
6. Add water and sprinkle with salt before whisking it together.
7. Sprinkle the oil around in the skillet to cover the rim.
8. Fill the skillet with the beaten egg.
9. Choose a combination of swirling and tossing to scramble the eggs, being sure to pull in all of the ingredients from the pan's sides.
10. Heat the eggs until they are no runnier.
11. Switch off the heat in the skillet.
12. Cover tortillas with beaten egg, steamed vegetables, and feta cheese on a level surface. Roll securely to close and eat!

Chapter 2: Greek Appetizers and Snacks

2.1 Healthy Greek Appetizer Platter

Cooking Time: 35 minutes
Serving Size: 6
Ingredients:
- 4.2 oz. breadsticks
- 4.2 oz. mini bruschetta
- 14 oz. pita bread
- 1 (7 oz.) can dolmas
- 8 oz. hard Greek cheese
- 1 long fresh baguette
- 6 oz. cherry tomatoes
- 2 large bell pepper
- 6 mini seedless cucumbers
- 1 12 oz. roasted peppers
- 7 oz. feta block
- 1 (11.6 oz.) Kalamata olives
- 1 (12 oz.) pepperoncini
- 2 celery stalks
- 1 (12 oz.) marinated artichoke hearts
- 1 (11.6 oz.) green olives

Meze Spreads and Dips
- Spicy Feta Spread
- Skordalia Spread
- Melitzanosalata Spread
- Tzatziki Dip

Method:
1. Take a broad platter or sharp knife.

2. In little plates, insert the eggplant spreads, spicy feta spreads, and potato spreads plates or spoons on your board directly.
3. Organize the spreads around all of the other components so that the colors are nicely scattered.
4. In order to do this, there is no wrong or right path. Only try to stop putting all the green vegetables next to each other.
5. The same for orange. To each mix, add micro spoons so that your guests can quickly scatter each dip.
6. Keep the rest of the baked goods (pita, bruschetta, grilled bread, and breadsticks) to not dry.
7. Just before eating, warm pita bread and cut it into pieces.

2.2 Greek Salad Skewers

Cooking Time: 25 minutes
Serving Size: 12

Ingredients:
- 12 cherry tomatoes
- 1 cucumber
- Freshly ground black pepper
- 12 pitted Kalamata olives
- 1 big block of feta
- 1 tablespoon parsley
- Flaky sea salt
- ¼ cup extra-virgin olive oil
- 1 clove garlic
- 1 tablespoon dill
- 1 tablespoon lemon juice

Method:
1. To make the feta marinade, mix the feta, olive oil, lime juice, cloves, dill, and parsley in a small cup.
2. Season with salt, then mix in the sauce until the cheese is fully wrapped.
3. Enable for fifteen minutes of resting time.
4. Pour feta, olives, grape tomatoes, and cucumber onto large forks to make skewers.

2.3 Greek-inspired Snack Board

Cooking Time: 40 minutes
Serving Size: 20

Ingredients:
Dip
- ½ teaspoon black pepper
- 1 pinch red pepper flakes
- 2 cloves garlic
- 1 teaspoon dill weed
- 6 ounces feta cheese
- 4 ounces cream cheese
- 1 tablespoon lemon juice
- 1 tablespoon Greek seasoning
- ⅓ cup Greek yogurt

Snack Board
- 6 ounces blackberries
- 4 ounces chickpeas
- 8 ounces pepperoni
- 1 can roasted almonds
- 1 jar pickled cauliflower
- 1 package pita chips
- 8 ounces salami
- 1 can artichoke hearts
- 1 English cucumber
- 1 box wheat crackers
- 1 jar pickled okra

- 20 baby carrots
- 2 red bell peppers
- 1 container hummus
- 1 jar Kalamata olives
- 1 basket cherry tomatoes
- 2 cups red grapes
- 14 ounces Cheddar cheese

Method:
1. In a mixing bowl, mix feta cheese, cream cheese, yogurt, lime juice, Greek spice, garlic, tarragon, and garlic powder.
2. Blend until fully smooth.
3. Serve in a bowl of red pepper flakes on top.
4. In small separate two bowls, put pickled cabbage, black olives, marinated okra, hummus, and onions.
5. On a broad cutting board or platter, arrange the bowls.
6. Fill the bowls halfway with Cream cheese, onions, oranges, broccoli, celery, bell peppers, tortilla chips, crackers, pepperoni, salami, almonds, blueberries, and chickpeas.
7. Refrigerate extra materials in sealed containers so you can restock the board as required.

2.4 Greek Garden Appetizer

Cooking Time: 15 minutes
Serving Size: 4

Ingredients:
- 2 tablespoons ripe olives
- Miniature pita pockets
- ¼ teaspoon pepper
- 1-½ cups cucumber
- 1 cup tomatoes
- ½ teaspoon garlic

- ¼ teaspoon oregano
- ½ cup green onions
- 2 cups feta cheese
- ¼ cup plain yogurt
- 1 carton garden cream cheese

Method:
1. Mix the sour cream, feta, yogurt, garlic, oregano, and peppers in a big mixing bowl.
2. Fill a 9-inch pie plate halfway with the mixture.
3. Over the cheese mixture, scatter the cucumber, onions, tomatoes, and artichokes.
4. Pita bread is a good component.
5. Keep leftovers refrigerated.

2.5 Feta and Greek Yogurt Pita Appetizer

Cooking Time: 30 minutes
Serving Size: 4

Ingredients:
- Fresh ground pepper
- 1 teaspoon olive oil
- Four tablespoons Greek yogurt
- 2-3 tablespoons mint
- 2 tablespoons crumbled feta
- 2 round medium pita bread

Method:
1. Preheat the oven to 400 degrees F.
2. Stir the feta with the yogurt in a medium bowl until smooth.
3. Mix in the mint and olive oil thoroughly.
4. Around each pita, distribute the yogurt-feta mixture.
5. Bake for about ten minutes, just until the tops of the pita begin to brown.
6. Remove the pitas and cut them into 6 or 8 pieces with a pizza cutter before serving.

2.6 Greek Layer Dip

Cooking Time: 20 minutes
Serving Size: 8
Ingredients:
- 2 tablespoons parsley
- Pita chips, broccoli, bell peppers, carrots
- ½ cup crumbled feta cheese
- ¼ cup Kalamata olives
- 1 tomato
- ½ cup seeded cucumber
- 1 container hummus
- ½ cup plain Greek yogurt

Method:
1. Place the hummus on the base of an 8x8-inch round roasting pan, a deep pie dish, or a specific glass baking dish in a smooth coat.
2. Spoonful, the Greek yogurt over the top with a tiny spoonful, then sprinkle lightly to make a fresh coat.
3. Spread the top of onions, cucumbers, feta, and olives.
4. Use clean parsley to scatter.
5. Put it in the fridge until prepared to eat, then mix as needed with crackers, pita chips, and diced vegetables.

2.7 Cheesy Greek Swirls

Cooking Time: 35 minutes
Serving Size: 12
Ingredients:
- ½ teaspoon pepper
- ½ teaspoon garlic powder

- 2 cups Swiss cheese
- ½ teaspoon salt
- 17 oz. frozen puff pastry
- 1 cup spinach
- 1 cup jarred red peppers
- 8-oz. cream cheese
- 1 cup Kalamata olives
- 1 cup artichoke hearts
- 1 cup feta cheese

Method:
1. Preheat the oven to 400 degrees Fahrenheit.
2. Puff pie should be thawed as per the package instructions.
3. Place one sheet of puff pastry on a solid floor and place half of the cream cheese mixture on it.
4. Part of the cheddar cheese, olives, artichokes, broccoli, red peppers, and Rye bread is layered.
5. Season with a quarter teaspoon of salt, powder, and garlic salt.
6. Shape a log by rolling the dough tightly.
7. Slice the logs into 1 inch thick slices and arrange them 1 inch apart on a cooking sheet lined with parchment paper.
8. Then using leftover dough and products, repeat the procedure.
9. Preheat oven to 400°F and bake for fifteen minutes, or until lightly browned.
10. Warm or at ambient temperature is fine. Any leftovers should be kept refrigerated.

2.8 Cool and Tangy Greek Snacks

Cooking Time: 5 minutes
Serving Size: 4

Ingredients:
- 1 teaspoon red peppers 8 woven

> wheat crackers
> - 8 teaspoon reduced-fat feta cheese
> - 8 cucumber

Method:
1. Add all the ingredients on top of the crackers.
2. It matches well with a Sauvignon Blanc bottle.
3. Mix and serve.

2.9 Greek Savory Snacks

Cooking Time: 50 minutes
Serving Size: 30
> **Ingredients:**
> - Pepper
> - Extra-virgin olive oil
> - 3 eggs
> - Salt
> - 2 packages of phyllo pastry
> - ½ lb. Cottage cheese
> - ½ lb. Feta cheese

Method:
1. Use the hands, crush the feta cheese and place it in a pan.
2. Cottage cheese, salt, and pepper, eggs, are added and blend until well mixed.
3. Place the Phyllo sheet on a broad workpiece and take one sheet at the moment.
4. On each, spray some sunflower oil.
5. At 356°F, turn on the stove.
6. At the start of a stripe, insert a teaspoon of the combination and then "cover" it, placing the extreme left end on the right-hand side.
7. Go forward and roll it into a triangle and place it on a baking sheet coated with paper towels.

8. Sprinkle some olive oil in the pan of all of them when done.
9. Bake for 20 minutes or before it turns golden.

2.10 Greek Burrito Snack Wrap

Cooking Time: 5 minutes
Serving Size: 2

Ingredients:
- ¼ cup cherry tomatoes
- 2 tablespoon feta cheese
- 2 tablespoon tzatziki sauce
- 2 whole wheat flour tortillas
- 2 eggs, beaten
- ¼ teaspoon oregano
- 1 cup baby spinach
- ¼ teaspoon salt and pepper
- 1 tablespoon olive oil

Method:
1. In a wide nonstick saucepan over medium heat, add the oil; add the eggs, salt, peppers, and oregano.
2. Lessen heat and add and cook, scraping the skillet's bottom and sides with a spatula as the mixture starts to shape big, soft curds.
3. Cook, constantly stirring, until the eggs have thickened to your liking.
4. Tzatziki sauce should be spread down the middle of each tortilla, leaving a 1 ½ -inch (2.5 cm) border at the left and right sides.
5. Add fried egg combination, onions, and feta cheese on top.
6. Cover the bottom of the flatbread over the stuffing, then pull in the sides; load up firmly from the edge.

2.11 Greek Salad Snack Skewers

Cooking Time: 25 minutes
Serving Size: 12

Ingredients:
- 12 cherry tomatoes
- 1 cucumber
- Freshly ground black pepper
- 12 pitted Kalamata olives
- 1 tablespoon fresh parsley
- Flaky sea salt
- 1 big block of feta
- 1 clove garlic
- ¼ cup extra-virgin olive oil
- 1 tablespoon lemon juice
- 1 tablespoon fresh dill

Method:
1. To make the feta marinade, mix the feta, canola oil, lime juice, cloves, dill, and tarragon in a small cup.
2. Add salt and pepper, then mix in the sauce until the cheese is fully wrapped.
3. Allow for fifteen minutes of resting time.
4. Layer feta, artichokes, grape tomatoes, and cucumber onto small forks to make skewers.

2.12 Saganaki Recipe

Cooking Time: 13 minutes
Serving Size: 2

Ingredients:
- ½ lemon, or to taste
- 1 tablespoon Italian parsley
- 1 tablespoon olive oil
- 2 tablespoons brandy
- 1 package kasseri cheese

- ¼ cup all-purpose flour
- 1 tablespoon water

Method:
1. Water should be brushed on both sides of the kasseri cheese.
2. Dredge all sides in starch, ensuring to cover the entire surface.
3. Steam a well-seasoned stainless steel skillet over medium-high heat until it begins to smoke.
4. Pour in the extra virgin olive oil.
5. Position the floured cheese in the hot oil with care.
6. Heat for about two minutes, or until the cheese starts to ooze and a light golden crust emerges.
7. With a spoon, quickly turn the cheese over. Fry till the bottom of the pan is nicely browned.
8. Remove the skillet from the heat and put it on a plate lined with tea towels.
9. Brandy should be poured over the cheese.
10. Then use a fireplace flame, light the brandy.
11. To put out the last few fires, pour some lime juice on edge.

2.13 Greek Stuffed Cucumber Bites

Cooking Time: 15 minutes
Serving Size: 12

Ingredients:
- Kosher salt
- Freshly ground black pepper
- 1 tablespoon olive oil
- 1 teaspoon oregano
- 4 large cucumbers
- Juice of 1 lemon
- 1 clove garlic
- 1-pint cherry tomatoes
- ½ cup crumbled feta
- 2 tablespoon chopped dill
- ½ cup Kalamata olives

Method:
1. Cucumbers should be sliced into 3" bits.
2. Make a well in each cucumber with a melon baller or a fork.
3. Toss together tomatoes, artichokes, feta, tarragon, lime juice, garlic, canola oil, and oregano in a big mixing bowl.
4. Salt and pepper to taste.
5. Cover cucumbers with salad combination.
6. If needed, top with more dill before serving.

2.14 Greek Tortilla Pinwheels

Cooking Time: 15 minutes
Serving Size: 8

Ingredients:
- 0.25 teaspoon oregano
- Black pepper
- 5 black olives
- 0.25 green bell pepper

- 1 tortilla
- 1 tomato
- 0.2 cucumber
- 1.75 ounces feta cheese
- 3 tablespoons Greek yogurt

Method:
1. Arrange all of your items ahead of time.
2. Place the feta cheese and Greek yogurt combination on a tortilla on a surface or other dry worktop.
3. Keep a small border from around the surface clear.
4. The salad vegetables should be uniformly distributed around the cheese, followed by the oregano and peppers.
5. Cover the tortilla in bubble wrap and roll it up as tightly as possible.
6. Place in the fridge for about 30 minutes to firm up.
7. Remove the tortilla from the wrapper and cut it into 8 even pieces.
8. Layout flat on a tray to serve.

Chapter 3: Greek Lunch Recipes

3.1 Skordalia

Cooking Time: 1 hour
Serving Size: 4

Ingredients:
- 1 cup canned chicken broth
- 2 teaspoons dried oregano
- 3 boneless chicken breasts
- ½ pound ziti
- 4 ounces feta cheese
- 1 tablespoon lemon juice
- 1 teaspoon salt
- ½ teaspoon fresh-ground black pepper
- 3 tablespoons fresh parsley
- 1 ½ cups cherry tomatoes

Method:
1. Boil the chicken stock and the oregano in a large skillet once half a cup of liquid is left in the dish, about three minutes.
2. Mix in the cubes of chicken, protect and withdraw the pan from the flame.
3. In the cooking liquid, let the meat heat until just cooked, about eight minutes.
4. Heat the ziti until cooked, about 13 minutes, in a big pot of hot, salted liquid.
5. Flush and mix the pasta with the meat, feta, lime juice, pepper, salt, and coriander mixture.
6. Stir until you have fully melted the cheese. Drop the cherry tomatoes down.

7. Mix and serve hot.

3.2 Greek Chicken Rice Bowl

Cooking Time: 20 minutes
Serving Size: 4
Ingredients:
Greek Marinade
- 1 teaspoon kosher salt
- ½ teaspoon black pepper
- 2 teaspoon minced garlic
- 1 ½ tablespoon dried oregano
- ¼ cup extra-virgin olive oil
- ½ tablespoon red wine vinegar
- ¼ cup fresh lemon juice

Rice Bowl
- Hummus
- Family Bowls white rice
- 1 medium red onion
- 1 cup crumbled feta cheese
- 12 boneless skinless chicken thighs
- 4 tomatoes
- 1 cup Kalamata olives
- 2 cups seedless cucumbers

Method:
1. Transfer the dressing components to a large mixing bowl to blend properly. Save ½ of the filling in an enclosed jar.
2. Transfer the remaining dressing to a big plastic sealed plastic chicken thigh package.
3. Cover the bag and rub the chicken with the marinade. If needed, put it in the fridge for several hours.

4. Over a medium-high flame, heat a skillet, then sleet a bit of sesame oil into the pan.
5. To extract excess sauce, pat the chicken thighs with a clean cloth and cook the chicken, about 4-5 minutes each side, until crispy and fried through.
6. Remove the chicken from a dish to cool whereas the other components are cooked.
7. Put down and cut the cucumber, cabbage, peppers, and olives together.
8. Microwave rice cups and divided equally between 4 cups according to box instructions.
9. Add a few feta slices of cheese, cucumbers, onions, tomatoes, and olives to each cup.
10. Add a spoonful of cream cheese to the cups and add 2-3 pieces of chicken per dish.
11. If needed, eat with whole wheat pita or tortilla.

3.3 Quick and Healthy Greek Salmon Salad

Cooking Time: 12 minutes
Serving Size: 4

Ingredients:
For Salad
- Kalamata olives
- Quality Greek feta cheese
- 8 oz. Romaine lettuce
- 1 English cucumber
- 2 shallots
- 1 bell pepper
- 10 oz. grape tomatoes

For Salmon

- Dried oregano 1 ½
- Salt and black pepper
- 1 lb. salmon fillet

For the Lemon-Mint Vinaigrette
- 1 teaspoon oregano
- ½ teaspoon sweet paprika
- 2 garlic cloves
- 30 fresh mint leaves
- 2 large lemons
- ½ cup extra virgin olive oil

Method:
1. Heat the oven around 425 degrees F and put a rack in the center.
2. Get the salmon seasoned. On all sides, brush the fish dry and sprinkle with kosher salt, peppers, and dried oregano.
3. Organize on a lightly greased sheet pan and apply olive oil to clean the surface of the fish.
4. Cook the salmon for 12 to 15 minutes in the hot oven until it has finished and flakes instantly.
5. Focus on the salads and the vinaigrette in the meantime. Have the salad packed.
6. Transfer the lettuce, onions, green peppers, cucumbers, parsley, and Kalamata olives into a large salad dish.
7. Make the vinaigrette primed.
8. Apply the olive oil, lime juice, garlic, new mint, oregano, and parmesan to the small food processor equipped with a blade.
9. Insert a tablespoon of black pepper and sea salt. Blend until well-combined.
10. Over the salad, add around ½ of the vinaigrette. To mix, flip. Now put on top the cubes of feta cheese.

11. Create bowls for your fish salad. Switch the salad to four serving cups, and finish each with one piece of fish.
12. Sprinkle on top of the salmon with the leftover vinaigrette.

3.4 Mediterranean Orzo Salad Recipe

Cooking Time: 10 minutes
Serving Size: 6

Ingredients:
- 2 teaspoons capers
- Feta cheese
- ½ cup fresh dill
- ¼ cup Kalamata olives
- ½ green bell pepper
- 1 cup fresh parsley
- 1 ½ cup orzo pasta
- 2 green onions
- 1-pint grape tomatoes

For the Dressing
- 1 garlic clove
- 1 teaspoon oregano
- 1 lemon zested
- ¼ cup extra-virgin olive oil

Method:
1. Make the orzo pasta per package directions. Drain and chill quickly.
2. Incorporate the cherry tomatoes, spring onions, bell peppers, coriander, dill, olives, and capers in a wide mixing dish.
3. Insert the pasta orzo. Get the dressing done.

4. Mix the lime juice, lime zest, olive oil, cloves, oregano, and coarse salt and pepper sprinkle to taste in a shallow cup. Whisk to blend.
5. Put the salad over the coating and swirl until thoroughly mixed, and the dressing is well covered with the orzo pasta.
6. Cover with creamy feta cheese bits. When serving, protect and chill in the fridge for a bit.

3.5 Melitzanosalata Recipe (Greek Eggplant Dip)

Cooking Time: 20 minutes
Serving Size: 6

Ingredients:
- Kalamata olives sliced
- Feta cheese
- 1 lemon zested
- ¼ cup extra-virgin olive oil
- 2 large eggplants
- ½ teaspoon ground cumin
- Pepper flakes
- 2 large garlic cloves
- 1 cup fresh parsley
- Kosher salt and black pepper
- ¼ red onion

Method:
1. Hold the eggplant whole and penetrate it in a few locations with a spoon.
2. Get the eggplant smoked.
3. Position the eggplant over a gas burner, barbecue, or under a broiler, and roast until the skin is

completely fried and the eggplant is very tender, flipping it around with a pair of tweezers.
4. Cool the eggplant and remove it. Put the eggplant in a pan and put it aside until it is cold enough to treat.
5. Slice off the burnt skin and discard it. Break the eggplant into pieces and put it in a colander to get out of any extra juices leftover.
6. To a mixing cup, pass the eggplant. Add the cabbage, coriander, lime juice, olive oil, and garlic.
7. Transfer salt and black pepper and seasoning. Mix to blend and divide the eggplant into smaller pieces with your fork.
8. At this stage, it is a smart idea to protect and cold the eggplant dipping in the refrigerator for a few short minutes if you have the opportunity.
9. To a serving dish, pass the eggplant dipping and scatter.
10. Toss in the olive oil. Garnish with lime zest, coriander, sweet onions, olives, and a feta sprinkle.
11. Use crumbly bread or flatbread to serve.

3.6 Greek Salad with Chicken

Cooking Time: 14 minutes
Serving Size: 2

Ingredients:
- ¼ cup Kalamata olives
- ¼ cup feta cheese
- 2 cups Mediterranean tomato salad
- 1 cup hothouse cucumber

- 6 cups lettuce romaine
- 1 8- ounce Chicken Breast

For the Greek Dressing
- ½ teaspoon kosher salt
- Freshly ground black pepper
- 2 teaspoons oregano
- 1 teaspoon sugar
- ¼ cup red wine vinegar
- 1 clove garlic
- ¼ cup extra virgin olive oil

Method:
1. For a large baking dish or two independent salad dishes, add the lettuce.
2. Cut the meat, tomatoes, salad, olives, cucumber, and feta cheese together.
3. Add the wine vinegar, olive oil, cloves, oregano, butter, salt, and black pepper to a small container to create the dressing.
4. Cover and move well with the cap until combined and mixed.
5. To satisfy, sprinkle with more salt and sugar and peppers.
6. Sprinkle over the salad with the dressing and mix to adjust.

3.7 Greek Chicken and Potatoes

Cooking Time: 45 minutes
Serving Size: 6

Ingredients:
For Chicken and Potatoes
- 12 Kalamata olives
- Fresh parsley

- 1 teaspoon black pepper
- 1 lemon
- 1 cup chicken broth
- 4 gold potatoes
- 1 medium yellow onion
- 3 lb. chicken pieces
- Salt

For the Lemon-Garlic Sauce
- 1 ½ tablespoon dried rosemary
- ½ teaspoon ground nutmeg
- ¼ cup lemon juice
- 12 fresh garlic cloves
- ¼ cup extra-virgin olive oil

Sides
- Tzatziki Sauce
- Pita Bread
- Greek Salad

Method:
1. Heat the oven to 350°F.
2. Pat clean chicken and carefully sprinkle with salt.
3. Organize the top of a baking dish or plate with fried potatoes and vegetables.
4. Dress with one teaspoon of salt and black pepper. Insert bits of chicken.
5. Take a sauce consisting of lemon-garlic. Stir ¼ cup of olive oil with lime juice, garlic powder, thyme, and nutmeg together in such a small mixing dish.
6. Over the chicken and potatoes, mix equally.
7. On edge, arrange the lemon wedges. Load the chicken stock from one hand into the saucepan.
8. Fry up for 45 minutes to one hour in an exposed warm oven until meat and vegetables are tender.

9. Turn off the heat and substitute, if you prefer, Kalamata olives.
10. Add a little bit of clean parsley to the garnish.
11. Present with Taztaziki salad and a piece of flatbread, if you choose.

3.8 Quick-Roasted Tomatoes with Garlic and Thyme

Cooking Time: 30 minutes
Serving Size: 6

Ingredients:
- Extra-virgin olive oil
- Crumbled feta cheese
- 1 teaspoon sumac
- ½ teaspoon chili pepper flakes
- Kosher salt and black pepper
- 2 teaspoon thyme
- 3 garlic cloves
- 2 lb. smaller tomatoes

Method:
1. Heat the oven to 450°F.
2. In a wide mixing cup, put the tomato pieces.
3. Add the chopped garlic, salt, peppers, seasoning, and clean thyme.
4. Sprinkle with a decent amount of extra virgin olive, around ¼ cup or so. Toss it to coat it.
5. Use a rim to move the tomato to a baking tray. Place the tomatoes, flesh lengthways in one single sheet.

6. Grill for 30 minutes to an hour in your hot oven just until the tomatoes have fallen to your desired thickness.
7. Withdraw from the heat. Feel free to serve it with more fresh thyme and a few splash of feta cheese if you intend to eat it soon.
8. Enjoy it at ambient temperature or hotter.

3.9 Greek-Style Baked Feta Recipe

Cooking Time: 30 minutes
Serving Size: 6

Ingredients:
- Fresh mint leaves
- Crusty bread
- Extra-virgin olive oil
- 8 oz. feta cheese
- ½ teaspoon red pepper flakes
- 4 fresh thyme sprigs
- ½ cup cherry tomatoes
- 2 teaspoon oregano
- ½ red onion
- ½ green bell pepper

Method:
1. Preheat oven to 400 degrees F and modify a tray in the center.
2. Organize the onions, green peppers, and grape tomatoes at the lower part of a ramekin or stove dish.
3. Spray some of the new thyme with 1 teaspoon oregano, chili flakes, and apply most of it. Drizzle some extra-virgin olive oil with it.
4. On top of the prepared vegetables, add the feta.

5. Prepare the leftover dried oregano with both the feta cube, a touch of chili flakes, and whatever is left of the fresh thyme.
6. Sprinkle the feta with a thick layer of olive oil and ensure to rub some of the butter on the edges.
7. Position the baking sheet on the oven's center rack and bake for 20 minutes.
8. Serve it with tortilla chips or Spanish toasted bread.

3.10 Greek Bowls with Roasted Garbanzo Beans

Cooking Time: 45 minutes
Serving Size: 4

Ingredients:
- 1 cup cherry tomatoes
- 1 lemon
- ½ cup Kalamata olives
- ½ cup feta cheese
- 1 pound fresh baby spinach
- 1 English cucumber
- 2 teaspoon chili powder
- 1 teaspoon ground cumin
- 1 (14.5 ounces) can garbanzo beans
- 1 tablespoon olive oil
- 2 (6-8 ounce) chicken breasts

Marinade
- 2 garlic cloves
- 1 lemon
- ¼ teaspoon pepper
- 2 teaspoons dried oregano

- ½ cup Kalamata olives
- ½ teaspoon salt
- ½ cup white wine or chicken stock

Method:
1. Mix in a big zip lock bag with all the marinade ingredients.
2. Chicken breasts are added. Stock for thirty minutes or up to eight hours in the refrigerator.
3. Preheat the oven to 400°.
4. Drain the garbanzo bean and wash them. Pat with a clean cloth to rinse.
5. Break the zip lock bag and transfer meat, and remove the marinade.
6. Sprinkle with one tablespoon olive oil in a wide baking sheet.
7. Place one half of the dry garbanzo bean and put the meat on the other.
8. Spray the chili powder and cilantro with the garbanzo bean.
9. Add a dash of pepper and salt. Transfer to the garbanzo bean an extra teaspoon of coconut oil and shake.
10. Cook the chicken and bean for about 30 minutes at 400° or until the chicken is cooked completely.
11. During baking, toss beans each time.
12. Before moving them to your boxes, cool fully.
13. Align boxes. In one side of the box, put ¼ of the spinach.
14. On the other, meat. Divide the remaining ingredients similarly.

15. Load the Tzatkiki dressing into a little bowl and store it in the fridge.

Chapter 4: Greek Dinner Recipes

4.1 Grilled Eggplant Pita Pizzas

Cooking Time: 40 minutes
Serving Size: 4

Ingredients:
- ½ teaspoon red pepper flakes
- 1 cup basil leaves
- ¾ cup fresh mozzarella cheese
- ¼ cup pitted ripe olives
- 4 whole pita bread
- 1 large tomato
- 3 tablespoons olive oil
- ¼ teaspoon pepper
- 2 small eggplants
- 1 medium onion
- 12 garlic cloves
- 1 large sweet red pepper
- 1 teaspoon salt

Method:
1. Split the ¾-inch pieces of eggplant.
2. Position it over a sheet in a saucepan; season with salt and flip.
3. Enable thirty minutes to stand.
4. In the meantime, in a cup, toss one tablespoon of oil with red pepper, garlic, and onion.
5. Shift to a griddle or clear grill basket for grilling; put on the grill rack.
6. Barbecue, exposed, 8-12 minutes over a moderate flame or until veggies are finely charred and crunchy, stirring regularly.

7. Rinse the eggplants and drain them; dry them with towels.
8. Rub one tablespoon of oil with the eggplants; spray with pepper.
9. Grill, sealed, 4-5 minutes on either side until it is soft, over a moderate fire.
10. Break into quarters for each piece.
11. Brush the pita bread on both edges with the remaining butter.
12. Grill, sealed, for two minutes over medium-high heat or until the bottoms are finely browned. Retract from the fire.
13. Layer the grilled pitas with grilled peppers, onions, olives, and cheese.
14. Sprinkle with pepper seasoning if necessary.
15. Return to the grill; cook three minutes, covered, or until the cheese is melted.
16. Toss basil with that too.

4.2 Garlic-Grilled Chicken with Pesto Zucchini Ribbons

Cooking Time: 55 minutes
Serving Size: 4

Ingredients:
- ¼ teaspoon salt
- 4 boneless skinless chicken breast
- 4 garlic cloves
- ½ teaspoon ground pepper
- 2 tablespoons lemon juice
- 2 teaspoons lemon zest

Zucchini Mixture

- ¼ cup prepared pesto
- 4 ounces fresh mozzarella cheese
- ¼ teaspoon red pepper flakes
- ¼ teaspoon ground pepper
- 2 garlic cloves
- ¼ teaspoon salt
- ¼ cup sun-dried tomatoes
- 1 teaspoon olive oil
- 4 large zucchini

Method:
1. Blend the first five ingredients in a large pan.
2. Use chicken to insert; shift to cover. Let the 15 minutes stay.
3. In the meantime, trim the ends of the zucchini for the noodles.
4. Cut the zucchini down the middle into thin, small strips using a bread slicer or filet knife.
5. Break the zucchini on both sides until the beans become apparent, like peeling a potato.
6. Dump and save the seeded part for another use.
7. Cook chicken barbecue, wrapped, over medium heat or 4-inch broil.
8. A thermometer reads a thermometer inserted into the chicken from 4-5 minutes of heat on either side or until 165°. Take from the grill; load up.
9. Heat the vegetables and olive oil in a large nonstick bowl.
10. Add the garlic, cinnamon, flakes of pepper, and salt; boil for thirty seconds and mix.
11. Insert zucchini; fry and mix for three minutes or until soft and crispy.
12. Withdraw from the heat. Stir the pesto in.

13. Get the chicken sliced into strips. With zucchini noodles, eat. Cover with mozzarella cheese.

4.3 Grilled Eggplant with Feta Relish

Cooking Time: 25 minutes
Serving Size: 8

Ingredients:
- ½ teaspoon pepper
- Minced fresh basil
- 2 tablespoons olive oil
- 1 teaspoon salt
- 3 tablespoons balsamic vinaigrette
- ¼ cup chopped red onion
- 8 slices eggplant
- 1 teaspoon garlic powder
- ¾ cup peeled cucumber
- ½ cup plum tomato
- 1 cup crumbled feta cheese

Method:
1. Whisk the vinaigrette and herb powder together in a small bowl when blended.
2. Add the feta, cucumber, basil, and onions and mix.
3. Refrigerate before serving wrapped.
4. Brush with the oil on the eggplant; scatter with salt and black pepper.
5. Grill 4 inches, sealed, over medium-high heat or griddle.
6. Heat on either side for 4-5 minutes or until mild.
7. Cover the feta combination with eggplant. Scatter basil if needed.

4.4 Greek Beef Pitas

Cooking Time: 25 minutes
Serving Size: 4
   Ingredients:
- 4 whole pita bread
- Chopped tomatoes and cucumber
- ½ cup chopped cucumber
- 1 teaspoon dill weed
- 1 cup Greek yogurt
- 1 medium tomato, chopped
- 1 pound ground beef
- 1 teaspoon dried oregano
- ¾ teaspoon salt
- 3 garlic cloves
- 1 small onion

Method:
1. Cook meat, garlic, and onion in a frying pan over medium heat for ten minutes or until beef is no redder and veggies are soft, splitting meat into crumbles; clean.
2. Insert the oregano and half a teaspoon of salt.
3. Mix the yogurt, onion, cucumber, dill, and the leftover salt in a shallow dish.
4. Pour the mixture over each pita bread with ¾ cup meat combination; finish with two tablespoons of yogurt sauce.
5. Cover with optional tomatoes and cucumbers if needed. With the leftover yogurt sauce, eat.

4.5 Greek Brown and Wild Rice Bowls

Cooking Time: 15 minutes
Serving Size: 2

Ingredients:
- ¼ cup pitted Greek olives
- Minced fresh parsley
- ¾ cup cherry tomatoes
- ¼ cup crumbled feta cheese
- 1 package whole grain rice
- ½ medium ripe avocado
- ¼ cup Greek vinaigrette

Method:
1. Merge the rice mixture and two teaspoons of vinaigrette in a microwave-safe dish.
2. Wrap and cook for about two minutes until fully cooked.
3. Split into two bowls.
4. Cover with avocado, onions, olives, dairy, leftover seasoning, and parsley, if necessary.

4.6 Greek Sheet Pan Chicken Dinner

Cooking Time: 40 minutes
Serving Size: 4

Ingredients:
Marinade
- 2 teaspoons paprika
- 2 teaspoons oregano
- ½ teaspoon salt
- ¼ teaspoon pepper
- 4 tablespoons olive oil
- 4 garlic cloves

- 2 tablespoons lemon juice

For Veggies and Chicken
- ¼ cup Kalamata olives
- 2 whole lemons
- 1 pound mixed color potatoes
- ¼ cup crumbled Feta
- 4 Chicken breasts
- 1 red onion
- 10 whole garlic cloves
- 2 red peppers

Method:
1. Heat the oven to 400F.
2. Mix all the components in a shallow saucepan with the marinade.
3. Use a baking dish to put sliced vegetables.
4. Position the veggies in and around the meat.
5. Pour all the vegetables into the marinade and brush on the chicken.
6. Organize the mixture equally and nestle around the sheet pan with sliced lemons.
7. Put in the oven and bake for 30-35 minutes or until the chicken hits 165 degrees and the vegetables are slightly orange.
8. Squeeze over the fried dish with sliced lemons.
9. Spray with olive oil with grated cheese and Kalamata.

4.7 Grecian Chicken

Cooking Time: 30 minutes
Serving Size: 4

Ingredients:
- 2 tablespoons ripe olives

- Hot cooked orzo pasta
- 1 medium garlic clove
- ½ cup of water
- 1 tablespoon lemon-pepper seasoning
- 1 tablespoon Greek seasoning
- ½ cup chopped onion
- 1 tablespoon capers
- 3 teaspoons olive oil
- 2 medium tomatoes
- 1 cup fresh mushrooms
- 1 pound chicken tenderloins

Method:
1. Heat two teaspoons of oil over the moderate flame in a wide skillet.
2. Add the chicken; sauté for ten minutes until it is no longer pink. Remove it and keep it hot.
3. Heat and cook oil in the same pan; add the remaining ingredients.
4. For 2-3 minutes, continue cooking until the onion is transparent.
5. Stir in garlic; simmer for an additional two minutes. Insert water; put to a boil.
6. Reduce heat; boil, exposed, 3-4 minutes until the vegetables are tender.
7. Set the chicken back in the skillet; add the olives.
8. Simmer, uncovered, 2-minute before the chicken is cooked thoroughly. Present with orzo if needed.

4.8 Greek Tilapia

Cooking Time: 40 minutes
Serving Size: 4
Ingredients:

- 1 tablespoon lemon juice
- ⅛ teaspoon pepper
- ¼ cup pine nuts, toasted
- 1 tablespoon fresh parsley
- 1 large tomato
- ¼ cup chopped ripe olives
- 4 tilapia fillets
- ¼ cup fat-free milk
- ¼ teaspoon cayenne pepper
- 4 teaspoons butter
- ¾ cup crumbled feta cheese
- 1 large egg

Method:
1. Brown salmon in oil in wide cast iron or another ovenproof pan.
2. Integrate the egg, milk, cheese, and cayenne in a shallow saucepan and spoon over the fish.
3. Spray with onions, raw cashews, and olives.
4. Toast, exposed, 10-15 minutes at 425° before the fish only starts to blister easily with a spoon.
5. Mix the parsley, lime juice, and peppers in a shallow saucepan and sleet over the fish.

4.9 Greek-Style Stuffed Peppers

Cooking Time: 4-½ hours
Serving Size: 8

Ingredients:
- ½ teaspoon red pepper flakes
- ½ teaspoon pepper
- 2 tablespoons olive oil
- ½ teaspoon salt
- Chopped fresh parsley

- ½ cup Greek olives
- 1 cup cooked barley
- 1 cup crumbled feta cheese
- 1 can crushed tomatoes
- 1 pound ground lamb
- 1-½ teaspoons dried oregano
- 3 garlic cloves, minced
- 2 medium peppers
- 1 small fennel bulb
- 1 package frozen spinach
- 1 small red onion

Method:
1. Heat the oil over moderate heat in a large pan.
2. Insert fennel and onions; continue cooking for ten minutes until soft.
3. Add the garlic and veggies; cook for one minute longer. Mildly cool.
4. Break the peppers and save the tops; extract and discard the seeds.
5. Pour 1 cup of chopped tomatoes into the 6- or 7-quarter rim.
6. Combine the lamb, rye, 1 cup of feta cheese, olives, and spices in a large mixing bowl; add the mixture of fennel.
7. Mix the spoon into the peppers; place in a slow cooker.
8. Pour the remainder of the crushed tomatoes over the peppers; replace the tops with pepper.
9. Cook, wrapped, until peppers are soft, 4 to 5 hours on medium.
10. Serve with extra feta and minced parsley if needed.

4.10 Lemony Greek Beef and Vegetables

Cooking Time: 30 minutes
Serving Size: 4

Ingredients:
- 2 tablespoons lemon juice
- ½ cup Parmesan cheese
- 2 tablespoons minced fresh oregano
- ¼ teaspoon salt
- ¼ cup white wine
- 1 can navy beans
- 1 bunch baby bok choy
- 5 medium carrots
- 3 garlic cloves
- 1 tablespoon olive oil
- 1 pound ground beef

Method:
1. Cut and dispose of the bok choy root edge.
2. Chop the leaves thinly sliced. Break into 1-inch stalks. Now put aside.
3. Heat beef on moderate heat in a large pan until no longer pink, splitting into crumbles, 5-7 minutes; rinse.
4. Cover and set it aside from the skillet.
5. Heat the oil over moderate to high flame in the same pan.
6. Insert bok choy stalks and vegetables; continue cooking until crisp-tender, 5-7 minutes.
7. Boost heat to high; stir in cloves, bok choy leaf, and ¼ cup liquor.
8. Heat, stirring, until the leaves wilt, five minutes, to loosen the browned bits from the pot.

9. Incorporate ground beef, rice, oregano, salts, and ample residual wine to keep the mixture wet.
10. Stir in the juice from the lemon; scatter with the Parmesan cheese.

Chapter 5: Greek Salads

5.1 Greek Salad with Chicken

Cooking Time: 14 minutes
Serving Size: 2

Ingredients:
- ¼ cup Kalamata olives
- ¼ cup feta cheese
- 2 cups Mediterranean tomato salad
- 1 cup hothouse cucumber
- 1 8- ounce Greek chicken breast
- 6 cups lettuce

For the Greek Dressing
- 1 teaspoon sugar
- ½ teaspoon kosher salt and black pepper
- 1 clove garlic
- 2 teaspoons oregano
- ¼ cup red wine vinegar
- ¼ cup olive oil

Method:
1. In a large mixing platter or two separate salad bowls, put the lettuce.
2. Sliced meat, tomato bowl, cucumber, artichokes, and feta cheese are served on top.
3. In a small canning container, mix the canola oil, white wine vinegar, garlic, marjoram, sugar, and salt, and black pepper to create the dressing.
4. Cover with the cap and shake vigorously until well combined and mixed.
5. To taste, add more salt and sugar, and peppers.
6. Toss the salad with the seasoning and season to taste.

5.2 Greek Salad Recipe with Lemon Dressing

Cooking Time: 15 minutes
Serving Size: 4

Ingredients:
Greek Salad
- 2/3 cup feta cheese
- Garlic lemon vinaigrette
- ½ red onion
- 2/3 cup Kalamata olives
- 2 cups tomatoes
- 1 cucumber
- 1 head Romaine lettuce

Garlic Lemon Vinaigrette
- ¼ teaspoon salt
- ¼ teaspoon black pepper
- 1 teaspoon dried oregano
- ½ teaspoon sugar
- ½ cup olive oil
- 3 tablespoon red wine vinegar
- 2 garlic cloves
- 3 tablespoon lemon juice

Method:
1. Toss all components in a large mixing bowl with the required size of dressing until well combined.
2. Combine all ingredients in a mixing bowl and whisk until smooth.
3. If required, season with more salt and pepper.

5.3 Greek Salad with Edamame

Cooking Time: 20 mins
Serving Size: 4

Ingredients:
- ¼ cup Kalamata olives
- ¼ cup slivered red onion

- ½ cup feta cheese
- ¼ cup fresh basil
- 1 cup tomatoes
- ½ European cucumber
- ¼ cup red-wine vinegar
- 8 cups romaine
- 16 ounces edamame
- ¼ teaspoon salt
- ¼ teaspoon ground pepper
- 3 tablespoons olive oil

Method:
1. In a big mixing bowl, combine the vinegar, oil, pepper, and salt.
2. Toss in the iceberg lettuce, edamame, peppers, tomato, tzatziki, spinach, artichokes, and onion.

5.4 Chopped Greek Salad

Cooking Time: 30 minutes
Serving Size: 8

Ingredients:
Greek Salad
- ½ cup Kalamata olives
- 6 ounces feta cheese
- ½ medium red onion
- ½ cup fresh parsley
- 10 ounces romaine lettuce
- 1 medium cucumber
- 1 yellow bell pepper
- 1-pint cherry tomatoes

Greek Vinaigrette
- ½ teaspoon salt
- Pinch of red pepper flakes
- 2 teaspoons dried oregano
- 1 teaspoon honey syrup
- ¼ cup red wine vinegar

- 2 medium cloves garlic
- ½ cup olive oil

Method:
1. Mix the sliced lettuce, tomatoes, celery, peppers, onions, tarragon, olives, and feta in a wide serving dish.
2. Combine the components in a mixing bowl and set them aside.
3. Mix all of the components in a fluid measuring cup to produce the vinaigrette.
4. Mix until smooth.
5. If you want a tangier seasoning, add more vinegar; if you want a milder dressing, add more syrup.

5.5 Greek Pasta Salad

Cooking Time: 3 hours 30 mins
Serving Size: 8

Ingredients:
- ½ cup sliced black olives
- ½ cup feta cheese
- 1 red bell pepper
- ½ cucumber
- 2 cups penne pasta
- 1 small red onion
- 1 green bell pepper
- ¼ cup red wine vinegar
- ⅔ cup olive oil
- 10 cherry tomatoes
- 1 tablespoon lemon juice
- 2 teaspoons oregano
- Salt and pepper to taste
- 2 cloves garlic

Method:
1. Bring a big pot halfway with water and bring to the boil over medium temperature, lightly salted.
2. When the water boils, add the penne and bring it back to a boil.
3. Heat the pasta uncovered, mixing periodically, for 11 minutes, or until it is heated through and still strong to the touch.
4. Drain well with a colander placed in the sink after rinsing with cold water.
5. Combine the vinegar, lime juice, cloves, oregano, pepper, salt, and vegetable oil in a mixing bowl.
6. In a big mixing bowl, combine the spaghetti, tomatoes, onion, red and green beans, cucumber, artichokes, and feta cheese.
7. Combine the spaghetti and vinaigrette in a mixing bowl.
8. Before serving, cover and relax for 3 hours.

5.6 Ladolemono Greek Salad Dressing

Cooking Time: 10 mins
Serving Size: 2

Ingredients:
- ¾ teaspoon black pepper
- ¾ cup extra virgin olive oil
- 1 to large garlic clove
- ¾ teaspoon kosher salt
- 2 teaspoons oregano
- ¼ cup fresh lemon juice

Method:
1. In a mixing bowl, combine the lime juice, oregano, cloves, salt, and peppers.
2. To mix the ingredients, whisk them together.
3. Steadily drizzle in the olive oil when stirring vigorously.

5.7 Greek Salad with Lettuce and Lemon Garlic Dressing

Cooking Time: 20 mins
Serving Size: 4

Ingredients:
- Kosher salt
- Black pepper
- ½ teaspoon dried oregano
- 1 head romaine lettuce
- 3 tablespoons lemon juice
- ½ cup whole olives
- 4 tablespoons olive oil
- 1 clove garlic
- 1 medium cucumber
- ½ bell pepper
- ¾ cup feta cheese
- 1 large tomato
- 1 small onion
- 3 radishes

Method:
1. Collect the required components.
2. If the cucumber's skin is too thick, peel it.
3. It should be sliced into thin rounds.
4. Slice the tomato after cutting the stem and heart.
5. Cut the radishes and onion very finely.
6. Bell peppers can be sliced into strips.
7. In a large mixing bowl, mix the cucumber, cabbage, sliced bell peppers, and onion.
8. Combine the feta cheese and artichokes in a mixing dish.
9. Merge the olive oil, lime juice, cloves, and oregano in a small cup. To mix ingredients, whisk them together.
10. Toss the veggies in a bowl with lemon juice and vegetable oil.

11. Place sliced lettuce in separate salad bowls or sheets and top with the salad mixture.
12. Season with coarse salt and black pepper to taste.

5.8 Athens Greek Salad

Cooking Time: 10 minutes
Serving Size: 4

Ingredients:
- Feta cheese
- ¼ cup olive oil
- Coarse salt to taste
- White pepper to taste
- 2 tablespoons capers
- Greek oregano
- 1 large tomato
- ½ green bell pepper
- Kalamata olives
- 1 small red onion
- 1 cucumber

Method:
1. To make this dish, choose a medium-sized dish.
2. To make four bits, cut the tomatoes in half lengthwise, then in the quarter again.
3. Put in a mixing bowl. Put the cucumber in the bowl after peeling it and cutting it into ½ -inch sections.
4. Position the spring onions and green bell pepper in the bowl after slicing them. Toss in the olives.
5. Add the capers, marjoram, salt, and white pepper to taste.
6. On top of the veggies, sprinkle the feta cheese.
7. Mix thoroughly with a gentle drizzle of olive oil.

5.9 Greek Salad with Homemade Vinaigrette

Cooking Time: 5 mins
Serving Size: 8

Ingredients:
- ¼ teaspoon black pepper
- ½ cup olive oil
- ½ teaspoon dried oregano
- ¼ teaspoon salt
- 1 teaspoon Dijon Mustard
- 2 garlic cloves
- 1 lemon
- 1/3 cup red wine vinegar

Method:
1. In a mixing bowl, mix some of the components except the olive oil.
2. Slowly drizzle in the olive oil, constantly whisking as you pour until the dressing is caramelized.

5.10 Quick and Light Greek Salad

Cooking Time: 15 mins
Serving Size: 6

Ingredients:
- 1 cup crumbled feta cheese
- 6 black Greek olives
- 1 ½ teaspoons dried oregano
- Salt and pepper
- 3 large ripe tomatoes
- ¼ cup olive oil
- 4 teaspoons lemon juice
- 1 small red onion
- 2 cucumbers

Method:
1. Conjoin tomatoes, celery, and onions in a deep serving bowl or on a baking tray.

2. Season with salt and pepper and drizzle with oil, lime juice, oregano, and season with salt and pepper.
3. Toss the salad with feta cheese and artichokes. Serve the food.

Chapter 6: Greek Soups and Sides

6.1 Avgolemono: Greek Lemon Chicken Soup

Cooking Time: 35 minutes
Serving Size: 6

Ingredients:
- 2 large eggs
- Fresh parsley for garnish
- 2 cooked chicken breast pieces
- ½ cup lemon juice
- Extra-virgin olive oil
- 1 cup rice
- 8 cups chicken broth
- 2 bay leaves
- Salt and pepper
- 1 cup green onions
- 2 garlic cloves
- 1 cup celery
- 1 cup carrots

Method:
1. Add 1 tablespoon olive oil, heated on moderate in a big Dutch oven or large pot.
2. Toss in the carrot, fennel, and fresh basil, and cook for a few minutes before adding the garlic.
3. Boost the heat to medium and add the garlic broth and coriander seeds.
4. Reduce to low heat and cook for 20 minutes, just until the rice is soft.
5. In a medium cup, whisk together all the lime juice and whites to make the egg-lemon mixture.
6. Mix the sauce into the chicken soup until it's completely mixed.
7. Remove the pan from the heat as soon as possible.

8. If desired, garnish with grated parmesan.
9. Serve with your favorite bread while it's still sweet.

6.2 Kakavia

Cooking Time: 50 minutes
Serving Size: 6
Ingredients:
- 2 tablespoons parsley
- 7-8 cups of water
- Salt and pepper
- Lemon wedges
- 2 pounds whole white fish
- 3 potatoes
- 1 canned tomato
- 1 celery stalk
- 2 garlic cloves
- 1 small onion
- ¼ cup olive oil

Method:
1. Fill a pot halfway with water and add the fish. Spray lightly with salt.
2. Bring to a boil, then reduce to low heat for 20 minutes.
3. Remove the fish to a serving platter and drain the broth to remove any remaining fish bones.
4. After wiping down the bowl, add onion, canola oil, and fennel.
5. Heat until soft over moderate flame.
6. Sprinkle with salt and insert the potatoes.
7. Heat for ten minutes over the moderate flame with the pureed tomato.
8. Take the stock to a boil, then remove it from the fire.

9. Turn the heat down to medium-low and continue to cook until the vegetables are tender about 15 minutes.
10. Transfer the fish to the broth after it has been cut into pieces.
11. Serve with lemon wedges and almond butter, garnished with parsley.

6.3 Kotosoupa

Cooking Time: 90 minutes
Serving Size: 8

Ingredients:
- 2 carrots
- Salt and pepper
- 2 large eggs
- Juice of 1 lemon
- 5 cups of water
- 200g short-grain rice
- 1 red onion
- 1 chicken

Method:
1. Clean the chicken carefully and put it in a large pan to make this typical Greek lemon chicken noodle soup.
2. Place the pot on medium temperature, cover, and bring to the boil; reduce the heat to low and cook the chicken for 1 hour and ten minutes.
3. Take the chicken out of the broth and rinse it.
4. In a bowl, heat the broth, add the rice, sprinkle with salt, and cook until the rice is cooked.
5. Crack an egg into a bowl and stir until soupy to make the egg-lemon liquid for this Greek citrus chicken noodle soup.
6. Pour a ladle of hot soup into the mixing bowl and whisk rapidly.

7. Insert another spoon of milk and whisk to warm the eggs.
8. While the soup is still hot, serve it with a side of Greek curry chicken.

6.4 Pattas

Cooking Time: 40 minutes
Serving Size: 4
Ingredients:
- Salt and pepper
- 1 small chili pepper
- 600 gram of pork leg
- 2 lemons
- 500 gram of pork belly

Method:
1. Start by washing the meat and cutting the pork belly into very small cubes.
2. Cut the pork leg into four pieces so that it will fit in the pot.
3. Clear the kettle, refill it with fresh water, bring it back to a boil, and add the poultry.
4. Hold it on the stove for 2 to 3 hours.
5. Return the meat to the pan, boneless, season with salt, spice, the juice of two lemons, and the chili peppers.
6. Start to boil for 30-40 minutes, stirring regularly to ensure that it gets everywhere.

6.5 Fasolada

Cooking Time: 80 minutes
Serving Size: 6
Ingredients:
- A pinch of paprika
- Salt and pepper

- 130ml olive oil
- 2 tablespoon tomato paste
- 500g dry white beans
- 1 large white onion
- 3 stalks of celery
- 4 carrots

Method:
1. Position the beans in a frying pan with enough cold water to cover them to make the fasolada.
2. Bring to the boil, then reduce to low heat and cook for 30-35 minutes, or until somewhat tender.
3. Slice the onions, celery, and vegetables thinly. In a large pan, heat 3-4 tablespoons of canola oil, then add the remaining vegetables and blend.
4. Sauté for two minutes, then add the tomato sauce and cook for another minute.
5. Cover and cook the fasolada for approximately 35 minutes, just until the beans are soft.
6. Load in the leftover olive oil and sprinkle with salt at the end of the cooking period.

6.6 Revithia

Cooking Time: 110 minutes
Serving Size: 5
Ingredients:
- 2 tablespoon flour
- Vegetable stock
- Salt and pepper
- Juice of 2 lemons
- 1 bay leaf
- 2 tablespoon dried oregano
- 1 large red onion
- ½ a cup olive oil
- 500g dry chickpeas

Method:
1. Wash the chickpeas and remove the soaked water when prepared to make this Greek chickpea pasta dish.
2. Wash the chickpeas thoroughly in a colander that has plenty of water.
3. Fill a wide pan halfway with cold water to cover the revithia.
4. Increase the heat to high and bring to a boil.
5. Wipe the chickpeas, then return them to the bowl with enough hot water to cover them fully.
6. Reduce the heat to low heat and cover the pot.
7. Enable the revithia to cook for 1-2 hours, based on the size of the chickpeas.
8. Sprinkle with salt as you slowly pour the combination into the pan with the chickpeas.
9. Mix the soup slowly for 2-3 minutes or until it softens.

6.7 Youvarlakia

Cooking Time: 40 minutes
Serving Size: 4

Ingredients:
For the Meatballs
- A pinch of coriander
- Freshly ground pepper
- 3 tablespoon fresh dill
- 1 teaspoon salt

- 500g lean beef
- 2 tablespoon olive oil
- ½ carrot
- ¼ of a cup rice
- 1 medium-sized onion
- 1 egg
- ½ cup parsley

For the Egg Lemon Sauce
- Juice of 2 lemons
- 2 eggs

Method:
1. Begin to make the meatballs for this Greek sausage soup.
2. In a large mixing bowl, combine all of the meatball components and whisk until soft, squeezing the components with your arm.
3. Enable fifteen minutes for the combination to rest in the refrigerator.
4. 2 1/2 cup water, brought to a boil in a big saucepan.
5. Reduce the heat to low and carefully drop the meatballs into the water.
6. Crack an egg into a bowl and stir to make the egg-lemon salsa for the Greek meatball broth. Whisk in the lime juice thoroughly.
7. Pour a ladle of hot soup into the mixing bowl and whisk easily.
8. Add another ladle and swirl until all is well mixed.
9. Toss the youvarlakia soup with the egg cream sauce.

6.8 Psarosoupa

Cooking Time: 55 minutes
Serving Size: 4

Ingredients:

- Juice of 1 lemon
- 2 tablespoon parsley
- 120ml olive oil
- 600g fish fillets
- 3 carrots
- 1.25 liters water
- 1 tablespoon salt
- 10 peppercorns
- 6 parsley stalks
- 2 celery stalks
- 1 red onion
- 2 potatoes
- 1 leek

Method:
1. In a wide saucepan over medium heat, combine the carrots, fennel, leek, garlic, onions, coriander seeds, and tarragon stalks, as well as the water.
2. Season with salt and pepper.
3. Fill a new pot with the stock and strain the vegetables through a fine sieve onto a plate, removing the peppercorns and tarragon stalks.
4. Return half of the vegetables to the stock and smash with a fork.
5. Enable the soup to rise to a boil before adding the olive oil and salmon fillets.
6. Cook for 20-30 minutes before adding the lime juice.
7. Remove from the heat after stirring.
8. Put the cooked vegetables and fish parts in individual bowls with the soup and serve right away, coated with finely grated parmesan.

6.9 Magiritsa

Cooking Time: 70 minutes
Serving Size: 8

Ingredients:
For the Magiritsa
- ½ a cup olive oil
- Salt and pepper
- 5 tablespoon fresh dill
- ½ cup rice
- 1kg lamb offal
- 5–6 spring onions
- 3 medium romaine lettuce
- 1 large red onion
- Intestines from 1 lamb

For the Egg Lemon Sauce
- Juice of 2 lemons
- 2 eggs

Method:
1. Wash and clean the organs completely before preparing this ancient Greece magiritsa dish.
2. Carry the organs as well as plenty of water on the stove in a big pot.
3. Caramelize the organs for five minutes in boiling water. Add the intestines and continue to blanch for another five minutes.
4. Heat the oil, minced veggies, and meat in a large saucepan over medium heat.
5. Put the pan on and add the finely chopped lettuce, pressing it down to match.
6. In a separate cup, whisk the egg whites with a hand mixer until they are foamy and heavy.
7. Slowly pour the yolk combination into the egg whites when stirring.
8. While the magiritsa is still soft, ladle it into cups.

6.10 Traditional Greek Lentil Soup

Cooking Time: 1 hour 20 minutes
Serving Size: 4

Ingredients:
- 1 teaspoon olive oil
- 1 teaspoon red wine vinegar
- 1 tablespoon tomato paste
- Salt and black pepper
- 1 pinch rosemary
- 2 bay leaves
- 1-quart water
- 1 pinch oregano
- 1 medium onion
- 1 large carrot
- ¼ cup olive oil
- 1 tablespoon garlic
- 8 ounces brown lentils

Method:
1. In a medium skillet, position lentils and enough water to make by 1 inch.
2. Bring a pot of water to a boil, then simmer for ten minutes before draining.
3. In a small saucepan, heat the olive oil.
4. Cover and mix in the garlic, carrot, and onion for about five minutes, or until the onion has hardened and become transparent.
5. In a large mixing bowl, combine the lentils, 1-quart water, marjoram, thyme, and garlic cloves.
6. Season with salt and pepper after adding the tomato sauce.
7. Cover and cook, stirring periodically, for thirty minutes, or until the lentils have weakened.
8. Add 1 teaspoon vegetable oil and 1 teaspoon white wine vinegar to fit.

Chapter 7: Greek Desserts

7.1 Traditional Greek Galaktoboureko

Cooking Time: 1 hour 45 minutes
Serving Size: 15

Ingredients:
- 1 cup water
- 1 cup white sugar
- ¾ cup butter, melted
- 12 sheets phyllo dough
- 6 cups whole milk
- ½ cup white sugar
- 1 teaspoon vanilla extract
- ¼ teaspoon salt
- 6 eggs
- 3 ½ tablespoons cornstarch
- 1 cup white sugar
- 1 cup semolina flour

Method:
1. In a medium skillet, bring the milk to a boil on medium-high heat.
2. Mix all the semolina, cornflour, 1 cup honey, and salt in a small bowl until there are no cornflour clumps.
3. Eggs should be whisked at high speed in a big mixing bowl.
4. Toss in ½ cup sugar for ten minutes, or until smooth and pale.
5. In a large mixing bowl, whisk together the scrambled eggs and apply them to the hot semolina combination.
6. Preheat the oven to 400 Fahrenheit.
7. Brush each sheet of phyllo with oil as you put it in the bowl with the custard.

8. In a roasting tin, bake for 35 to 40 minutes, just until the top layer is crispy and the sauce filling has set.
9. Combine the leftover cup of sugar and water in a shallow frying pan.

7.2 Baklava Recipe

Cooking Time: 40 minutes
Serving Size: 18

Ingredients:
- 1 teaspoon vanilla extract
- ½ cup honey
- 1 cup water
- 1 cup white sugar
- 1 package phyllo dough
- 1 cup butter
- 1 teaspoon ground cinnamon
- 1 pound nuts

Method:
1. Preheat the oven to 350 degrees Fahrenheit.
2. Toss nuts with cocoa powder after they've been chopped.
3. To suit the pan, cut the entire stack in a quarter.
4. As you operate, cover the phyllo with a softened cloth to prevent it from drying out.
5. Butter 2 layers of dough and put them in the pan.
6. Place two sheets of flour, butter, and nuts on top as you go.
7. Slice diamond forms to the sides of the hole with a paring blade.
8. Baklava should be crispy and fluffy after around 50 minutes in the oven.
9. While the baklava is cooking, make the sauce.
10. Bring sugar and water to a boil until the sugar has melted.

11. Mix in the vanilla and honey. Cook for about 20 minutes on low heat.
12. Remove the baklava from the oven and pour the sauce over it right away. Cupcake papers can be used for serving.

7.3 Greek Honey Cake

Cooking Time: 1 hour 10 minutes
Serving Size: 12
Ingredients:
- ¾ cup water
- 1 teaspoon lemon juice
- 1 cup white sugar
- 1 cup honey
- 1 cup all-purpose flour
- ¼ cup milk
- 1 cup chopped walnuts
- 1 ½ teaspoons baking powder
- ¾ cup white sugar
- 3 eggs
- ¼ teaspoon salt
- 1 teaspoon orange zest
- ¾ cup butter
- ½ teaspoon cinnamon

Method:
1. Preheat the oven to 350 degrees Fahrenheit.
2. A 9-inch square pan should be greased and floured.
3. Stir to combine cooking powder, salt, spice, and orange rind in a large mixing bowl.
4. Softened butter and ¾ cup sugar once smooth and creamy in a wide mixing bowl.
5. One at the moment beat throughout the eggs. Add the walnuts and blend well.

6. Pour the batter into the pan that has been prepared.
7. Preheat the oven to 400°F and bake for thirty minutes.
8. Enable fifteen minutes for cooling before cutting into diamond shapes.
9. Then use a spoon, drizzle honey syrup over the cake.
10. To make the honey syrup, add honey, 1 cup sugar, and liquid to a frying pan.
11. Cook for five minutes on low heat.
12. Bring to a boil, then reduce to a simmer for two minutes.

7.4 Loukoumades

Cooking Time: 1 hour 30 minutes
Serving Size: 25

Ingredients:
- 4 cups vegetable oil
- 2 teaspoons cinnamon
- ½ cup honey
- ½ cup water
- 2 packages of active dry yeast
- 3 eggs
- 4 cups all-purpose flour
- 1 cup warm water
- 1 teaspoon salt
- ⅓ cup butter
- ¼ cup white sugar
- ½ cup warm milk

Method:
1. In a tiny bag, scatter the yeast over the hot water.

2. Allow sitting for five minutes, just until the fermentation softens and forms a fluffy foam.
3. Combine the hot milk, sugar, and pinch of the salt mixing bowl and whisk to absorb.
4. Add in the oil, eggs, and starch until the dough is smooth and fluffy.
5. In a frying pan, combine honey and ¼ cup liquid and bring to the boil over moderate flame.
6. Preheat the oil in a heavy or a medium skillet to 350°F (175 degrees C).
7. In a cup of water, put a heavy table or soup spoon above the batter.
8. Into another hot grease, drop the balls of dough.
9. Cook until lightly browned on edge, then flip and fry the other side for two or three minutes per dish in the hot oil.

7.5 Greek Skillet Orange Fillo Cake

Cooking Time: 2 hours 25 minutes
Serving Size: 12

Ingredients:
Syrup
- 1 teaspoon ground cinnamon
- 1 orange
- 1 ½ cups water
- 2 cups white sugar

Cake
- ½ cup white sugar
- 1 tablespoon baking powder
- 1 container Greek yogurt
- ¾ cup olive oil
- 3 oranges
- 5 eggs
- 1 package phyllo dough

Method:

1. In a small saucepan, mix 2 cups glucose, liquid, and spices.
2. Bring to the boil and cook for ten minutes on high heat.
3. Preheat the oven to 350°F (180°C).
4. Take the phyllo plates from the box and set them aside.
5. As you prepare the rest of the ingredients, let the broken phyllo dry out just a little.
6. In a food processor or blender, mix orange juice, lime zest, eggs, yogurt, olive oil, ¼ cup sugar, and icing sugar.
7. Mix at high speed for 2 minutes or until foamy.
8. Orange slices can be used to decorate the edge of the cake.
9. Bake for 45 minutes in an oven and bake until the surface is crispy and the filling is ready.
10. Put down for at least 1 hour, just until the syrup has absorbed the majority of the liquid.

7.6 Fried Greek Pastry with Honey and Nuts

Cooking Time: 1 hour 30 minutes
Serving Size: 12

Ingredients:
- 1 cup honey
- ½ cup water
- 1 tablespoon sugar
- Two 1-inch orange zest
- One 3-inch cinnamon stick
- 1 teaspoon fresh lemon juice
- 3 large eggs
- 3 tablespoons olive oil
- Pinch of salt
- 1 ½ cups all-purpose flour
- Vegetable oil for frying

- 1 cup walnuts
- Ground cinnamon

Method:
1. Take the honey, milk, butter, lime zest, bay leaf, and lime juice to a boil in a medium skillet.
2. In a medium mixing cup, whisk together the eggs, vegetable oil, and salt with a rolling pin.
3. Stir in the flour until you have a stiff, bushy dough.
4. Create 4-inch squares out of the string. Repeat with the rest of the dough.
5. Warm 2 inches of peanut oil to 360° in a big saucepan.
6. Bake 3 minutes over medium fire, rotating once, until golden brown.
7. Heat the sugar syrup again.
8. Transfer a few baked goods at a time to the honey syrup and switch to cover with tongs.
9. Move to a big mixing bowl and toss with chopped nuts and spices.
10. Repeat the process till all the pastries have been coated.

Conclusion

Greek cuisine is famed for its complex flavors, but it is also recognized as one of the world's healthful foods. The use of spices and herbs to produce globally famous dishes has been refined by Greek cuisine through time. Spices and herbs offer different advantages. A few common options include allspice, which can help improve the immune function and alleviate pain; antioxidant-rich oregano; and basil, an aid against stomach aches and inflammatory. In Greek cooking, pasta and bread are popular, rendering wheat a significant aspect of the food. Wheat, particularly whole grains, provides main nutrients like zinc, protein nutrients, B vitamins, and even fiber. Its crucial value is that three rules are based on the Greek meal: Balance, Moderation, and Variety. Greek food has these three basic principles, and thus it is rich in health benefits. If you are thinking of introducing Greek food into your daily life, go for it and try your best with these delicious recipes.

Printed in Great Britain
by Amazon